Rapping about
Animal homes

Bobbie Kalman

Crabtree Publishing Company

www.crabtreebooks.com

Created by Bobbie Kalman

For Emese Felvegi,

with thanks for helping me stay in touch with my first home

Author and Editor-in-Chief
Bobbie Kalman

Editors
Kathy Middleton
Crystal Sikkens

Photo research
Bobbie Kalman

Design
Bobbie Kalman
Katherine Berti
Samantha Crabtree
   (logo and front cover)

Print and production coordinator
Katherine Berti

Prepress technician
Katherine Berti

Illustrations
Barbara Bedell: pages 14, 20, 21
Jeannette McNaughton-Julich:
   pages 12, 15

Photographs
Corel: pages 5 (top), 6
Creatas: pages 5 (bottom right)
BigStockPhoto: pages 5 (bottom left),
   8 (top)
Photo.com: page 23 (beaver)
Other images by Shutterstock

Library and Archives Canada Cataloguing in Publication

Kalman, Bobbie
    Rapping about animal homes / Bobbie Kalman.

(Rapping about--)
Includes index.
Issued also in electronic formats.
ISBN 978-0-7787-2793-4 (bound).--ISBN 978-0-7787-2800-9 (pbk.)

    1. Animals--Habitations--Juvenile literature. I. Title. II. Series:
Rapping about--

QL756.K357 2012   j591.56'4   C2011-907711-6

Library of Congress Cataloging-in-Publication Data

Kalman, Bobbie.
Rapping about animal homes / Bobbie Kalman.
p. cm. -- (Rapping about--)
Includes index.
ISBN 978-0-7787-2793-4 (reinforced library binding : alk. paper) -- ISBN 978-0-
7787-2800-9 (pbk. : alk. paper) -- ISBN 978-1-4271-7908-1 (electronic pdf) -- ISBN
978-1-4271-8023-0 (electronic html)
    1. Animals--Habitations--Juvenile literature. I. Title.

QL756.K35519 2012
591--dc23

2011046212

Crabtree Publishing Company

www.crabtreebooks.com   1-800-387-7650

Printed in Canada/022012/AV20120110

Published in Canada
Crabtree Publishing
616 Welland Ave.
St. Catharines, Ontario
L2M 5V6

Published in the United States
Crabtree Publishing
PMB 59051
350 Fifth Avenue, 59th Floor
New York, New York 10118

Published in the United Kingdom
Crabtree Publishing
Maritime House
Basin Road North, Hove
BN41 1WR

Published in Australia
Crabtree Publishing
3 Charles Street
Coburg North
VIC 3058

Contents

Home is shelter

Animals are **living things** that move and **roam**,
but they all need to have a place called home.
Home is **shelter** from sun, rain, or snow.
Home is a safe place for babies to grow.
Homes help baby animals **survive**.
To survive means to stay alive.

These baby wolves are outside their **den**. When they see danger, they run back in.

4

Do you know?

Animals live
in shelters outside.
When they are hunted,
these are places to hide.
A shelter keeps them dry
and warm in bad weather.
These coyote pups
live in a shelter together.

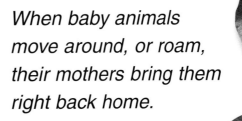

*When baby animals
move around, or roam,
their mothers bring them
right back home.*

Natural places

Forests, **grasslands**, **deserts**, and **lakes**,
are **habitats**, or natural places.
Some habitats are filled with trees and plants,
and others are wide open spaces.
Homes are in habitats, on the ground or in trees.
Some are in water—in lakes, rivers, and seas.

This cougar lives in a forest,
where many trees grow.
In wintertime, the trees and plants
are covered with snow.

This prairie dog's habitat is a grassland with flowers. These plants grow taller with the help of rain showers.

A desert is where this meerkat pup lives. The weather is hot and dry.

It does not rain much in this habitat. The sun shines high in the sky.

Dens in the wild

A den is an animal's home in the **wild**.

The "wild" is in nature. It is outside.

In their dens, animal babies hide.

They are safe from **predators**

while on the inside.

Safety and warmth are what dens provide.

The den of these baby mice is a hole in the ground.
They peek out of their den and then go back down.

A **cave** is a room between walls of rocks.

It makes a good den for this baby fox.

This cave is dry and big and wide.

A lot of fox kits can live inside.

A bat roost

Caves can be found in most habitats.

This dark cave is a **roost** for bats.

A roost is where bats sleep in a group.

Bats hang upside down. Their bodies droop.

There is a reason why they sleep this way.

Hanging makes it easier to fly away.

These bats are awake. They are ready to go.

Their wings are open, and their eyes are aglow.

Their glowing eyes create

quite a light show!

Bats fly through the night
to find food to eat.
Some bats eat fruits,
and others eat meat.

Digging deep

Burrows are tunnels under the ground.

A prairie dog burrow is called a **town**.

Towns have rooms for babies to sleep.

The tunnels and rooms are dug down deep.

room

tunnel

These prairie dog pups
stay safe in the ground
in case any predators
come sniffing around.
Their **prairie** grassland
has flowers and weeds
—the kind of food
a prairie dog needs.

Meerkats do not live alone.
They live in groups
in their desert home.
When some leave the burrow
to eat and play,
others stand guard—
so they won't become **prey**.

A **warren** is a burrow
under the ground.
In its joining tunnels,
bunnies move around.
Holes take the bunnies
above and below.
The bunnies know
where to come and go.

Beaver lodges

Lodges are homes that beavers make.

A lodge can be built on a river or lake.

Beavers make lodges from trees they chew.

Beavers are a busy building crew!

They also build dams to stop streams from flowing.

Their long, sharp teeth never stop growing.

Beaver lodges are built with care.
A hole at the top lets in air.

Under the water, the beavers swim
through tunnels that go out and in.
An extra tunnel allows escape
from predators that might make the mistake
of trying to get inside from the lake.
The beavers can get out in a hurry.
They will be safe. Do not worry!

Our nests are best!

"To make our **nests**, we use twigs and leave
but we don't just make our nests in trees.
Some of us build our nests on the ground,
and some of us build our nests upside down.
We are the best nest-makers around.
Who can we be? Just look and you'll see!"

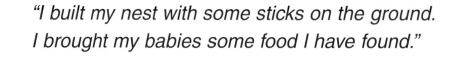

*"I built my nest with some sticks on the ground.
I brought my babies some food I have found."*

Upside down

"I am a weaver bird.
My nest hangs down.
This nest is green
but will soon turn brown.
I am a male bird
in search of a **mate**.
I build my nest
and then I must wait.
I wait for a female
to see my nest
and hope she will think
my nest is best.
She will then lay some eggs
in a bunch called a **batch**,
and from those eggs,
our **chicks** will **hatch**."

nest

Baby birds are called
nestlings *or chicks.*
They have hatched in a nest
made of leaves and sticks.

weaver chicks

17

Who else builds a nest?

What kind of animal makes a home called a nest?

Did you just guess "bird" and forget the rest?

What about turtles, ants, wasps, and bees—

and don't forget squirrels and orangutans, please!

Orangutan mothers make their nests high in trees.
They bend back some branches and pile on some leaves.

drey

ant

anthill or mound

Built in trees or on the ground, an ant's nest is called a **hill** or a **mound**.

hive

A squirrel's home is a nest called a **drey**. It's built high in a tree to keep predators away.

Hives are the nests of wasps and bees. Some build their hives in the branches of trees.

bee   wasp

Hibernation is a long winter sleep.

Hibernating animals do not wake up or eat.

Their bodies cool down,

and their hearts hardly beat.

A dormouse must eat a lot in the fall.
In winter months it will not eat at all.
It needs to gain a lot of weight
so it can survive on the food it ate.

This dormouse has started
its long winter rest.
It is curled up tightly
in its warm, cozy nest.